Art Therapy
Celtic

100 DESIGNS
COLOURING IN AND RELAXATION

illustrated by Michel Solliec

jacqui
small

First published in the UK, USA and Australia in 2015
Jacqui Small LLP
74–77 White Lion Street
London N1 9PF

Text © 2014 Jacqui Small LLP

First published by Hachette Livre (Hachette Pratique), 2014
© Hachette Livre (Hachette Pratique), 2013

Illustrations: Michel Solliec
Translation: Hilary Mandleberg

ISBN: 978 1 910254 07 3

10 9 8 7 6 5 4

Printed in China

Preface

Knots, triskelions, interlaced patterns and swirling spirals are the key motifs that together forged the identity of Celtic art. Expertise with a pair of compasses and an overwhelming taste for figurative art and visual complexity gave rise to an original art form where the artist's imagination really could run riot. Born at a time before writing was commonplace, Celtic art bears precious witness to the ancient Celts' way of thinking.

Celtic art began developing as early as the fifth century before Christ. Using indigenous and foreign motifs, the Celtic artisan constructed his design by blending depictions taken from the human, animal and vegetable kingdoms into one single whole. The results are novel forms and an allusive iconography that allow for an infinity of possible – no doubt often religious – readings.

In Ireland, this style of art survived the evangelisation of the fifth century A.D. and, in the form of the art of illumination, came to constitute one of the fundamental branches of Christian art.

The work that stands at the summit of this art form is the illuminated manuscript book of Gospels, the ninth-century *Book of Kells*, from which this book takes its inspiration. With its endless curves, spirals and interlaced patterns, the pages are saturated with symbols. They produce a hypnotic effect where pattern and background can no longer be distinguished from each other. In a society that was dominated by the oral tradition, the art of illumination offered people a visual compensation for the written word.

With the designs in this book, Michel Solliec invites you to plunge headfirst into an artistic world in perpetual motion and into an inexhaustible language of symbols.

Gaël Hily
Centre for Breton and Celtic Research,
University of Rennes 2

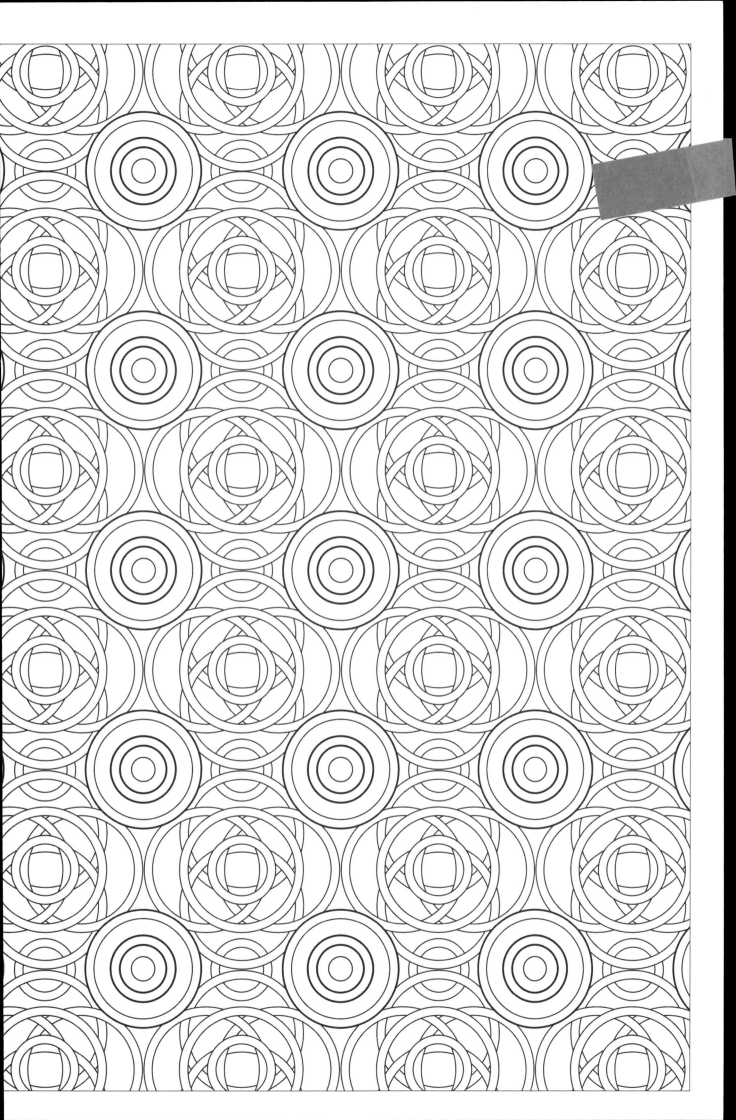

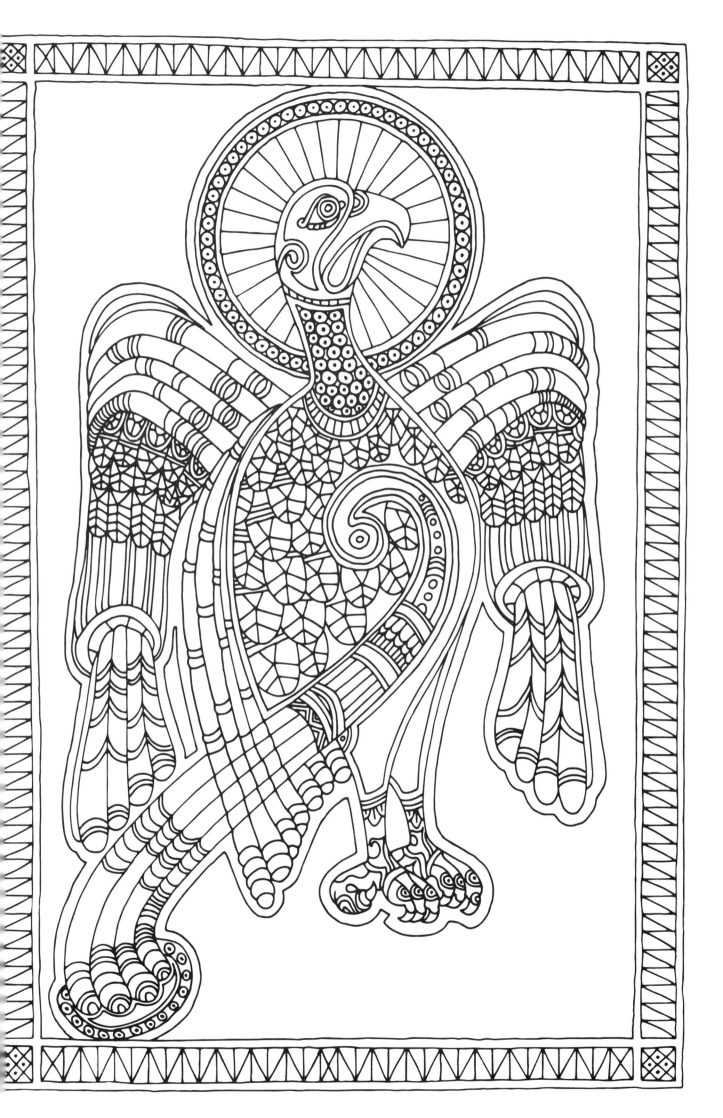

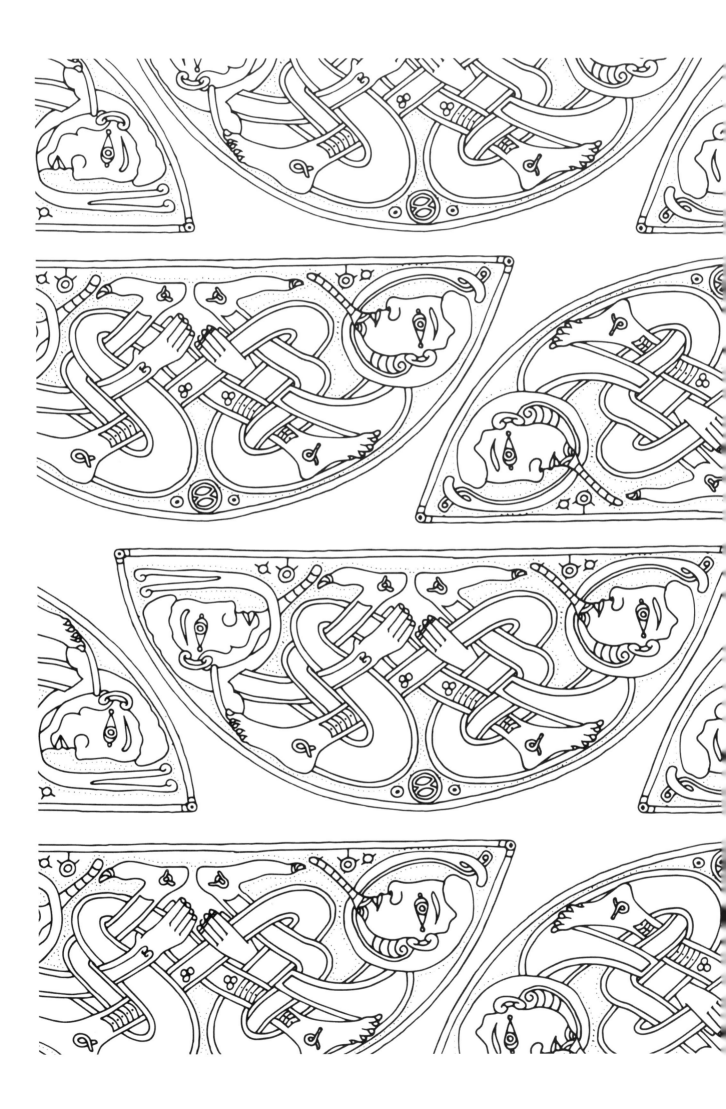

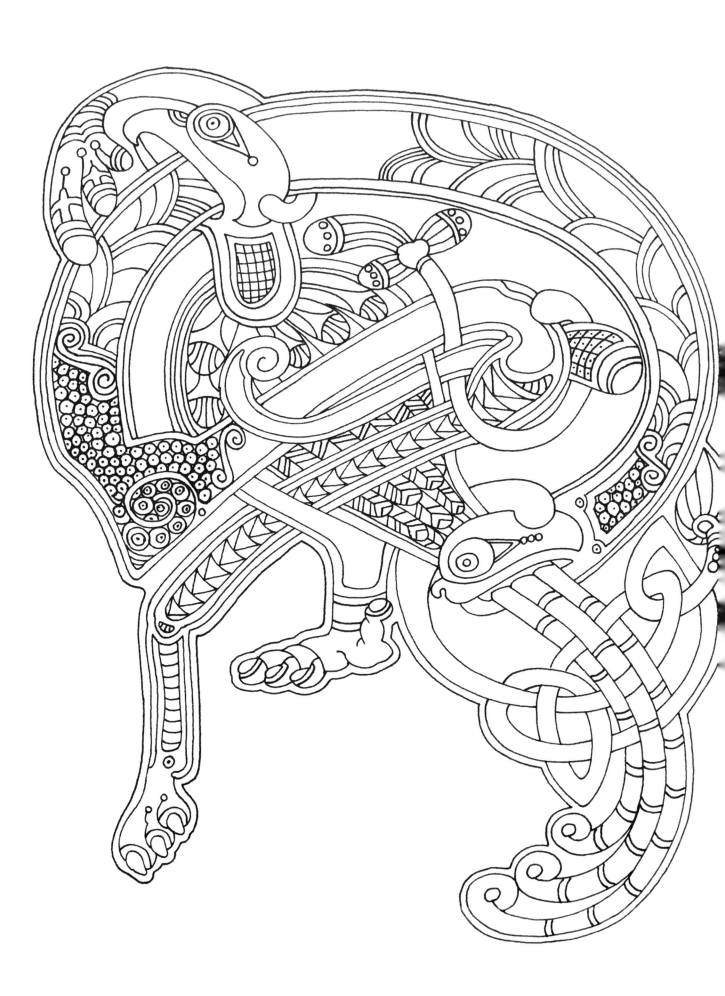

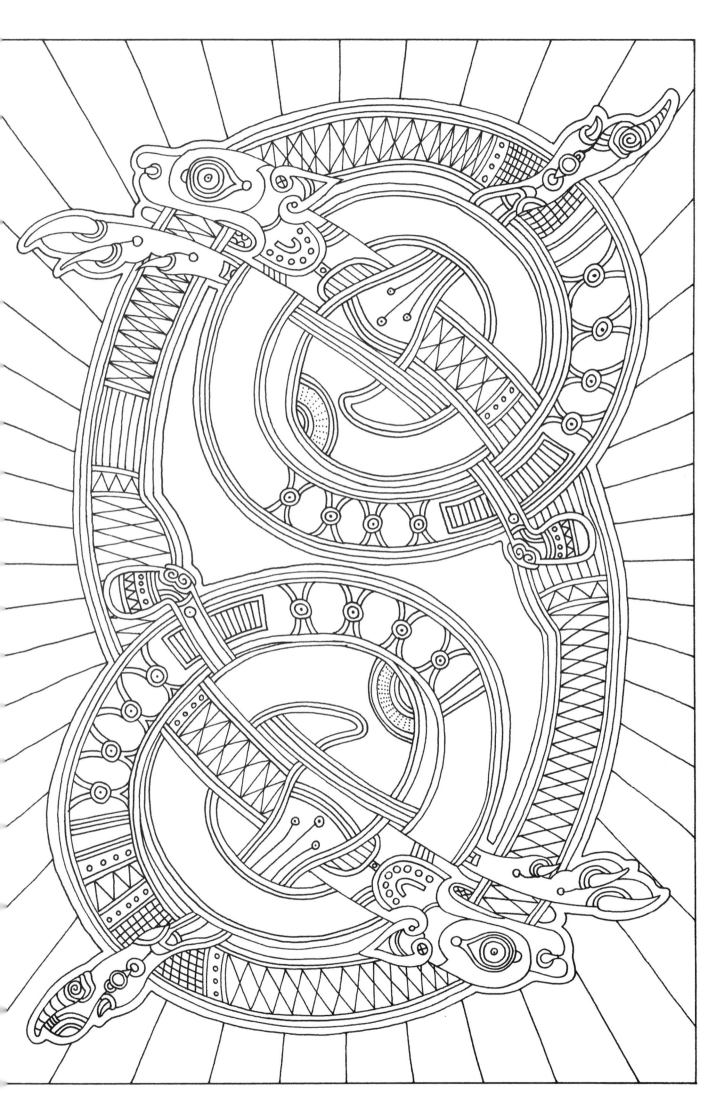

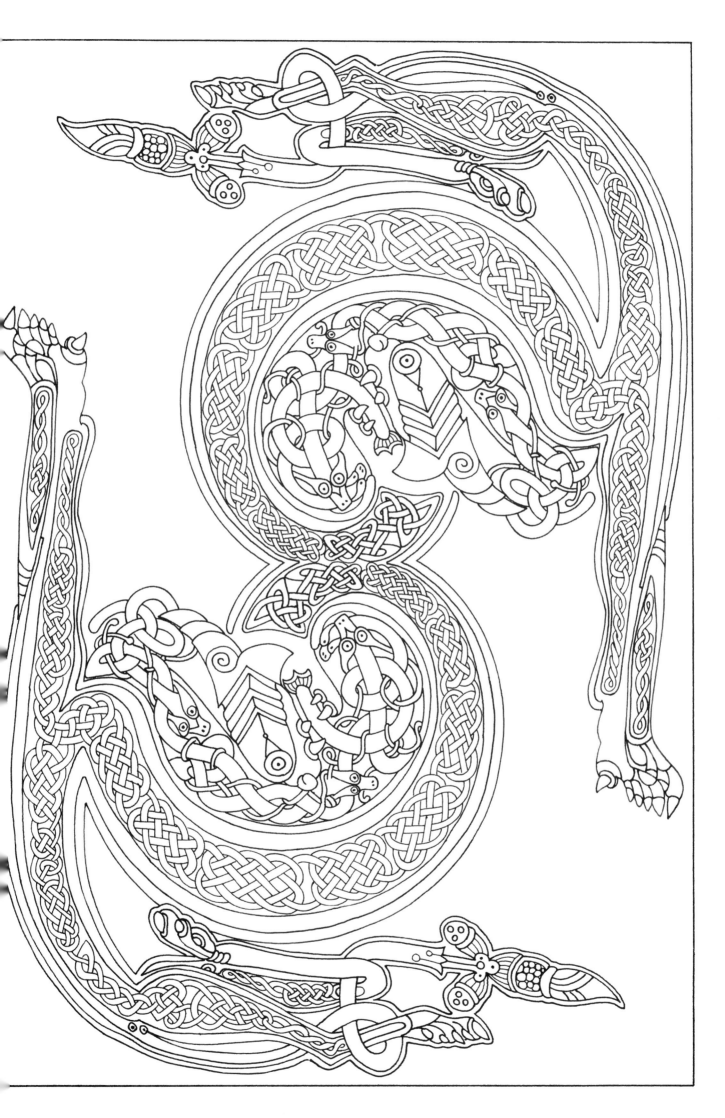

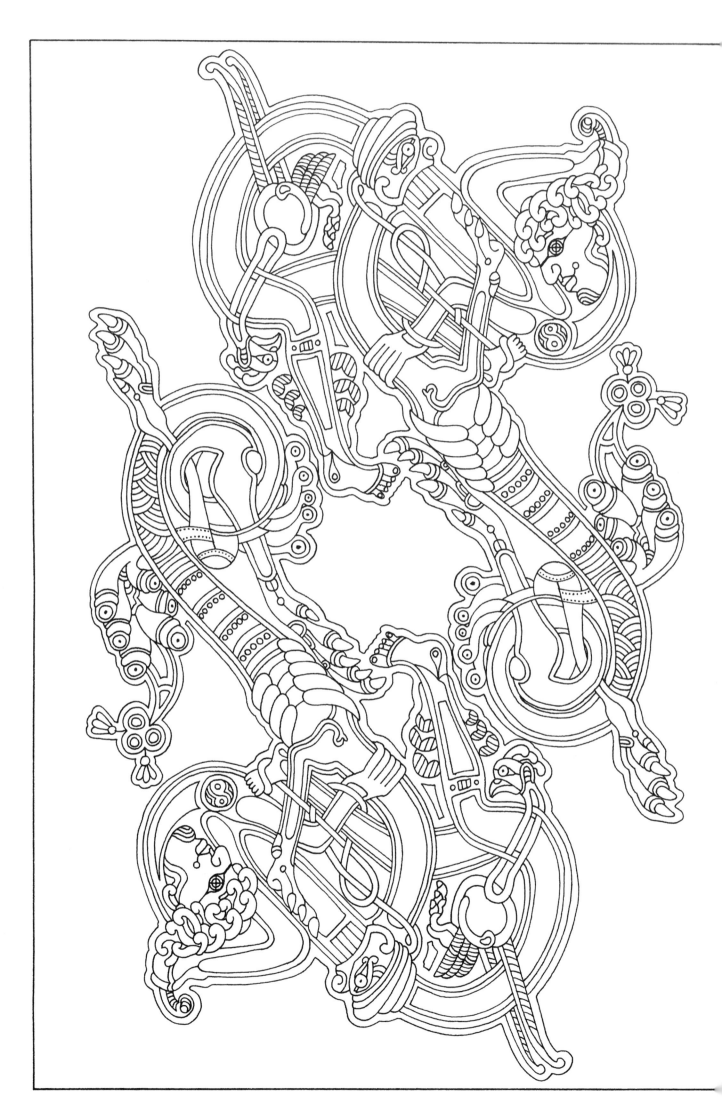

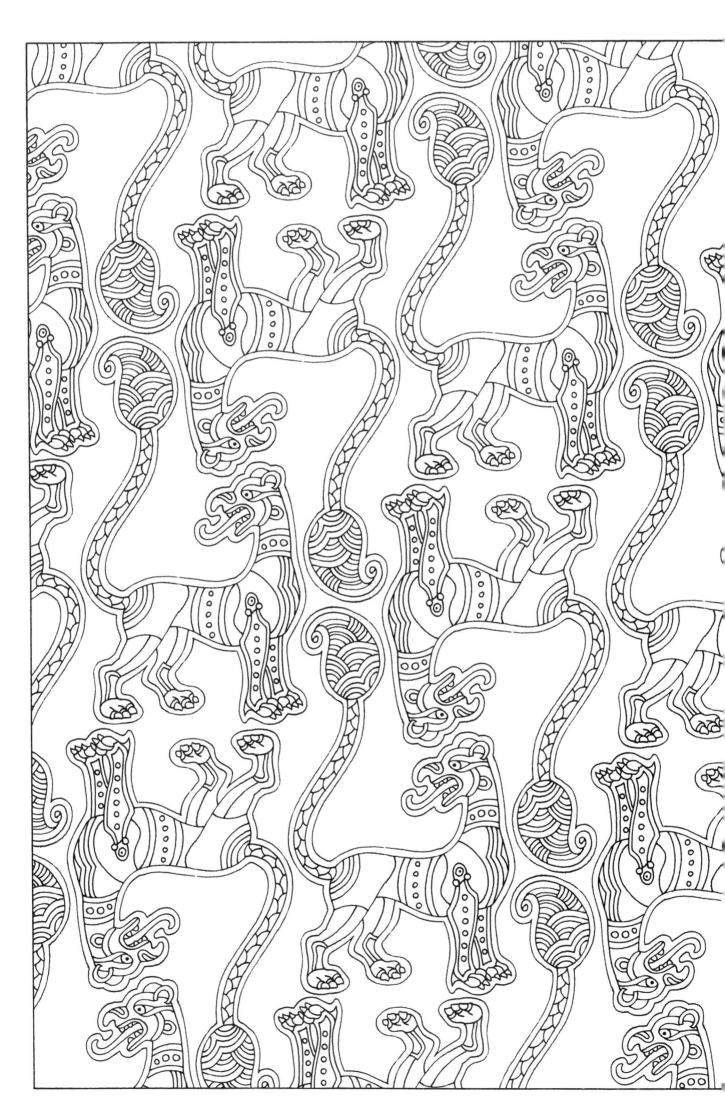